Nature-Inspired Innovations

NATURE-INSPIRED
CONTRApTIONS

Robin Koontz

Rourke
Educational Media

rourkeeducationalmedia.com

Before Reading:

Building Academic Vocabulary and Background Knowledge

Before reading a book, it is important to tap into what your child or students already know about the topic. This will help them develop their vocabulary, increase their reading comprehension, and make connections across the curriculum.

1. *Look at the cover of the book. What will this book be about?*
2. *What do you already know about the topic?*
3. *Let's study the Table of Contents. What will you learn about in the book's chapters?*
4. *What would you like to learn about this topic? Do you think you might learn about it from this book? Why or why not?*
5. *Use a reading journal to write about your knowledge of this topic. Record what you already know about the topic and what you hope to learn about the topic.*
6. *Read the book.*
7. *In your reading journal, record what you learned about the topic and your response to the book.*
8. *After reading the book complete the activities below.*

Content Area Vocabulary
Read the list. What do these words mean?

appendage
cuticle
exoskeleton
hexagrams
lithium-ion
microstructure
mollusks
polarization
polymer
receptors
silicone
superhydrophobic

After Reading:

Comprehension and Extension Activity

After reading the book, work on the following questions with your child or students in order to check their level of reading comprehension and content mastery.

1. *What kinds of contraptions have been inspired by biomimicry?* (Summarize)
2. *Why would material engineers be excited about the strength of a dactyl club?* (Asking Questions)
3. *Why does it take so long for a new design inspired by nature to be available to the public?* (Infer)
4. *What kinds of jobs do you see yourself doing in biomimicry? (*Text to Self Connection)
5. *Why are bio-inspired materials often healthier for the environment? (*Infer)

Extension Activity

Nature has many ways to collect water from dew and fog. Read about desert plants and animals. Then mimic an idea from nature to design a contraption to gather and/or store water. You might come up with an award-winning design!

Table of Contents

Bio-Fastening Systems

George de Mestral patented a toy airplane when he was only twelve years old. He continued to explore ideas for new inventions while working for an engineering company. One day while in the woods, George and his dog got covered in seedpods, called cockleburs.

While many types of plants have burrs, it was the thorny burr from a greater burdock plant that inspired George.

The purple flowers on a burdock appear mid-summer before the burrs form.

The inventor was intrigued at the relentless sticking power of the pods. He studied one under a microscope and discovered the pod's secret: it was covered with hundreds of tiny hooks. The hooks grabbed and stuck to loops of thread or fur.

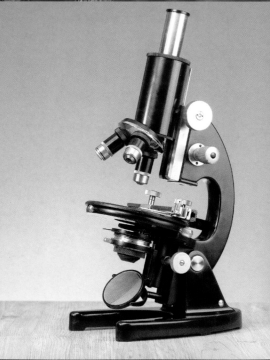

George designed a fastener system based on the cocklebur. He named his invention Velcro®, from two French words, *velour* and *crochet*. His creation, inspired by an annoying cocklebur, became one of the most famous examples of biomimicry in history.

George's Velcro® cotton fastener (right) was later constructed using nylon and polyester (below).

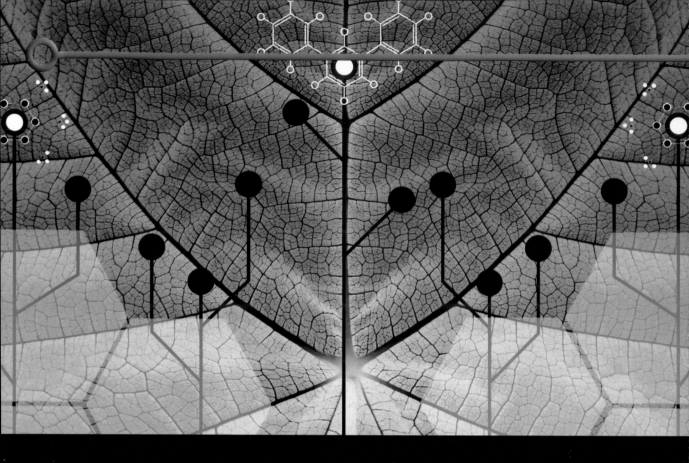

Everything that exists today in nature is the result of billions of years of evolution: tested against the elements and optimized by survival of the fittest. Nature is the world's largest science and engineering lab with 3.8 billion years of experience.

Biomimicry involves studying the way functions are delivered in biology and then translating that into designs that suit human needs. Scientists and engineers involved in biomimicry are often referred to as "biomimics"—people who learn from and attempt to mimic ways that nature has evolved to survive and thrive on Earth for millions of years.

They study and learn from nature to create innovative designs that help solve problems in our human societies and improve the world. All kinds of contraptions have been invented or improved upon thanks to nature's inspiration.

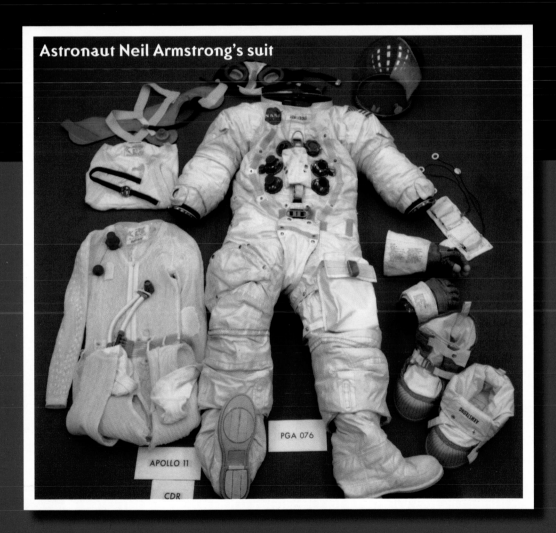

Astronaut Neil Armstrong's suit

APOLLO 11

CDR

PGA 076

Velcro® was first employed in the aerospace industry. The easy fastener helped astronauts get in and out of bulky space suits. It later caught on in sports and children's apparel and is now used in hundreds of products.

Cats are the inspiration for a variety of inventions. One is a new kind of thumbtack. A design engineer named Toshi Fukaya wanted to create a thumbtack that was painless to pick up or step on. He was inspired by a cat.

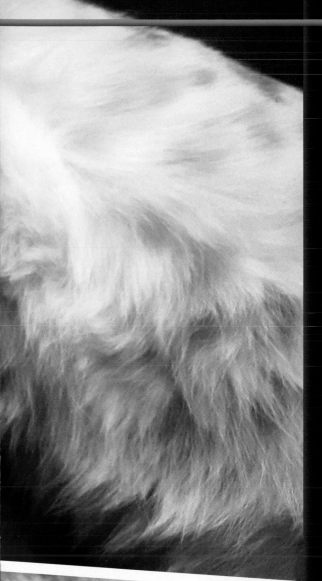

Unlike dogs, cats keep their claws inside a sheath until they decide to use them. Fukaya created a hollow **silicone** sheath that housed a sharp pin. When the silicone sheath was pushed to a hard surface, the pin emerged and stuck where it belonged. The pin withdrew when the sheath was removed. Fukaya won a design award for his cool invention!

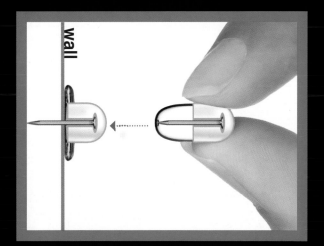

The Biomimicry Drawing Pin contains a sharp pin inside a bubble of silicone. The pin is exposed when it is pressed into a board or wall.

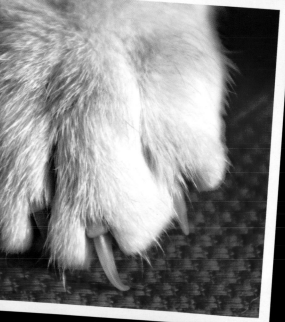

Nikola Tesla is famous for designing electricity supply systems. According to W. Bernard Carlson, a biographer, a cat named Macak introduced Tesla to electricity. He was petting his cat on a dry winter evening when he noticed sparks pop as he stroked. The static electricity fascinated Tesla, and could have been the spark that shaped his future in electricity.

Nikola Tesla
1856 — 1943

Gecko feet have also inspired several useful products. Geckos have millions of tiny adhesive foot hairs on each of their toes. Every square millimeter of a gecko's foot has about 14,000 hairs, called *setae*. Each of these hairs split into hundreds of even tinier tips.

tokay gecko

The incredible **microstructure** in each gecko foot can attach and detach with little effort. The feet can work on nearly any surface a gecko chooses to navigate, including underwater. And unlike slugs or snails, geckos leave no slime behind.

Researchers came up with a new invention based on gecko feet. They call it "Geckskin." This material is so strong, it can be used to attach and hold a heavy television to the wall. And it can easily be removed and reused. There are countless possible uses because of Geckskin's ability to stick to so many different surfaces.

A company called Felsuma is working to bring its version of Geckskin to the market soon.

> **❝**Geckskin will transform the way society, including consumers and engineers, thinks about attaching and releasing materials and surfaces.**❞**
> *Rana Gupta, CEO of Felsuma LLC*

Soft-bodied **mollusks** like the
octopus have also contributed many
ideas to biomimicry. An octopus uses
suction cups in its tentacles to grab prey
and pull it into its beaked mouth. It can
also cling to and climb rocky underwater

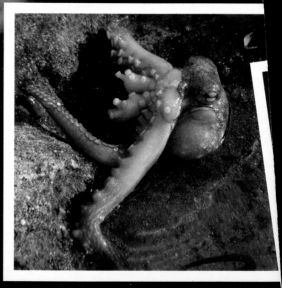

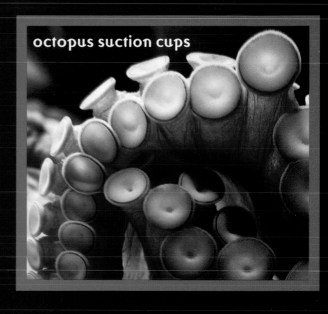

octopus suction cups

Researchers at Sungkyunkwan University in South Korea are studying how octopus suction cups work. The team's goal is to design an adhesive patch that performs the same way.

The patch would work on all kinds of wet or oily surfaces, from prickly and bumpy to glassy and smooth. It would also be easy and painless to remove. Researchers know that there would be a lot of uses for octopus-inspired adhesives.

Animal-Inspired Materials

Limpets, a type of marine snail, have teeth that may be the strongest biological material on Earth. The iron-bearing mineral in their tooth structures is called *goethite*. The structure of limpet teeth could perhaps be mimicked to manufacture environmentally friendly impact-resistant materials.

The muscular foot on a limpet is difficult to pry loose from its home.

Mollusks such as this snail are invertebrate animals—animals lacking a backbone—with a soft body that's often enclosed inside a shell.

Scientists have borrowed ideas from the way a mollusk grows its shell. They discovered that peptides, a chain of amino acids, have binding abilities that could improve **lithium-ion** (Li-ion) batteries.

goethite

Rechargeable lithium-ion batteries are used in most battery-powered electronic devices.

19

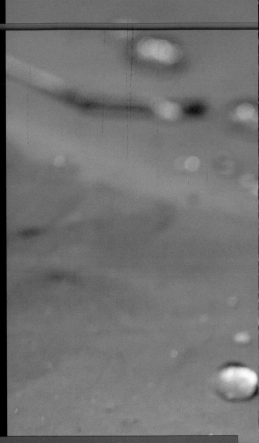

A lotus plant has textured, waxy leaves that are **superhydrophobic**. The leaves can repel and shed water. Researchers are studying ways to mimic the superhydrophobic qualities of a lotus leaf. They want to create highly water-repellent products for building as well as for other potential applications.

A lotus is a popular pond plant because of its beautiful flowers.

Scientists have invented a bio-inspired material that's possibly better than plastic. Recent research focused on the structure of an insect **cuticle**, which is their **exoskeleton**. The cuticle is composed of super-thin layers of chitin and protein. Chitin is a kind of natural **polymer**.

A cidada sheds, or molts, its exoskeleton in a process called ecdysis.

Chitin, such as that found in shrimp shells, is one of the most abundant organic materials on the planet.

Researchers in China were inspired

by fish scales and skeleton flowers when

they created a new kind of underwater surface

material. Underwater optics such as diving

Fish repel oil by trapping water in their scales. That makes the scales self-cleaning because oily things can't stick to them.

skeleton flower

The skeleton flower's white petals become transparent when they are wet. A loose cell structure in the petals causes the reaction.

The scientists combined the two systems. Their material repels oil and also turns transparent when wet.

Innovators looked at the structures of worms, fish, and snakes. They wanted ideas for a strong, flexible pipe system that would move raw materials through a factory. Steel pipes wore out quickly from abrasion from the products passing through them.

Snake structure inspired a strong, flexible hose that is lined with interlocking **hexagrams** made of ceramic. The hexagrams are separated by thin rubber barriers. The idea is being tested to replace steel pipes for certain applications, and it is working well!

hexagram

dactyl club

A variety of tiny, colorful mantis shrimp can pack a forceful wallop with its club-like **appendage**. Called the dactyl club, the shrimp can smash prey so fast and forcefully that it got the attention of material engineers.

Researchers studied the structure of the dactyl club and discovered why it was so strong and resilient. The outer layer had a crack-resistant layer that not only protected the club, but allowed the shrimp to do serious damage to whatever it punched.

A team led by engineer David Kisailus works with 3D printed models that mimic the structure of the dactyl club. They hope to learn new ideas to create lightweight, energy absorbing, and impact-resistant materials.

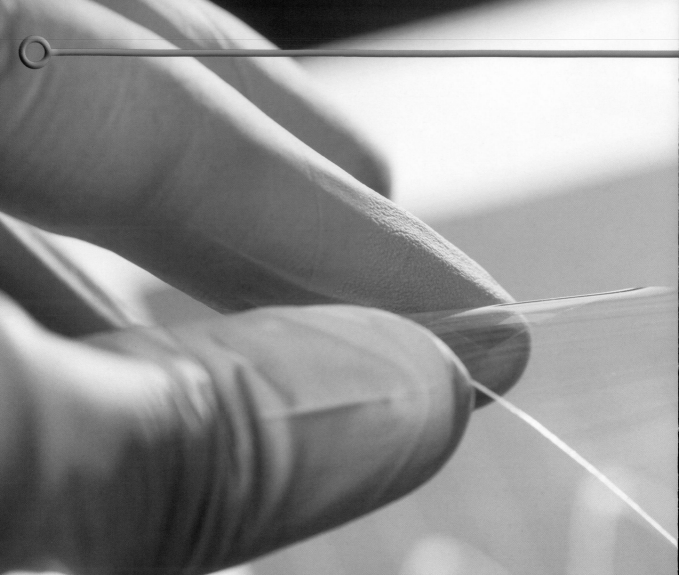

Eye-Inspired Products

Mantis shrimp can do more than smash things. Human eyes have three types of color **receptors**. But a mantis shrimp has 16, along with six **polarization** channels.

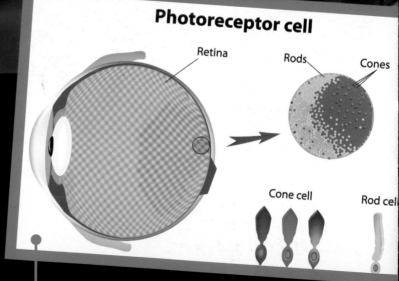

Photoreceptor cell

Retina

Rods

Cones

Cone cell

Rod cell

There are three color-sensitive cones in the retina of the human eye, acting as red-, green-, and blue-sensitive detectors.

Their highly sensitive eyes allow them to perceive images that are invisible to humans.

Mantis eyes inspired researchers to create a color-polarization camera. A camera that can see as well as a mantis shrimp could be used for early cancer detection, among other applications.

The eyes of a peacock mantis shrimp

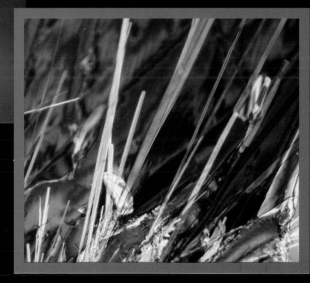

Polarized light is a contrast-enhancing technique that improves the quality of an image, such as in this microscopic shot of sodium carbonate microcrystals.

Bees have also inspired improvements for cameras. They rely on three extra eyes they have on top of the head to detect colors more directly. Researchers are studying this ability to design better sensors for drones, cameras, and robots.

Honeybees have three small eyes on the top of their heads called ocelli that are employed to navigate using sunlight.

Philippine bent-toed gecko

More ideas are being researched thanks to gecko eyes. Geckos have amazing night color vision. Engineers hope to develop better cameras and even multi-focal contact lenses based on gecko vision.

Night-vision devices are currently only monochrome. Their sensors create green visuals because human eyes are more sensitive to green light.

In the early 1980s, NASA scientists were inspired by eagle eyes to create protective glasses. They mimicked how eagle eyes produce tiny drops of oil that filter out harmful wavelengths. Eagle Eyes Optics now markets a full line of sunglasses based on the design.

Unlike typical sunglass lenses, Eagle Eyes lenses filter out harmful radiation, protecting the eye while enhancing eyesight. The lenses reduce light scattering while intensifying harmless wavelengths of light so that the vision is brighter and sharper.

Helping Aids

The plants and insects of the desert are designed to collect water from the air. An engineer named Pak Kitae, from South Korea, designed a fog-collecting bottle inspired by a native dew collector called a fog beetle.

Dew drops collect on the ridges of the beetle's shell. The beetle points its rear up and the water streams down to its mouth. Kitae's invention, called a Dew Bank bottle, even looks a little bit like a beetle.

The steel dome becomes colder than the air in the morning. Dew drops form on the steel ribs in the dome. The collected water slides down the ribs into a channel around the base, collecting several ounces of water in a single desert night.

It is expected that this device could gather enough moisture for a full glass of water per use.

An unusual little animal from Asia and sub-Saharan Africa inspired a collapsible backpack. The Pangolin Bag was designed to mimic the overlapping scales of the cat-sized pangolin. The brand's purpose is to honor nature as inspiration. The backpack is made using recycled rubber tubes.

Pangolin backpack

There are eight known species of pangolins. They are being poached by the millions for their meat and scales. Their status ranges from Vulnerable to Critically Endangered.

Modern intermittent windshield wipers are adjustable to "blink" fast or slow, depending on how much wiping is needed.

Blinking eyelids inspired intermittent windshield wiper systems. Robert Kearns got the idea in 1953 when he was hit in the eye by a champagne cork, which blinded him. The engineer mimicked the opening and closing abilities of an eyelid to design a pausing windshield wiper. The system is still used in vehicles today.

There are many varieties of raised pavement markers today, including vibration lines, Botts' dots, road studs, road turtles, cat's eyes, and RRPMs (retroreflective raised pavement markers).

Cats inspired road reflectors on the highway. In 1934, an English road contractor named Percy Shaw wanted to improve on ways to make roads easier to navigate in the dark.

Cats, dogs, and deer have a layer behind the retina that reflects light, called the tapetum lucidum.

The device he designed reminded him of the eye-shine of cat eyes when they seem to glow in the dark. He even nicknamed his invention "cat's eyes." Versions of his feline-inspired safety design are all over the world today.

Earth provides a wealth of ideas to create or improve the function of just about anything. Humans just have to figure out how best to be inspired by the vast knowledge and experience that nature has to offer them.

> **❝** Biomimicry is about going back to our roots. When we have a problem to solve, we have to ask ourselves, 'What would nature do?' **❞**
>
> *Tom Tyrrell, founder of*
> *Great Lakes Biomimicry*

Glossary

appendage (uh-PEN-dij): a projecting part of an invertebrate or other living organism, with a distinct appearance or function

cuticle (KYOO-tuh-kuhl): a protective and waxy or hard layer covering the outside of a plant, invertebrate, or shell

exoskeleton (ek-soh-SKEL-uh-tuhn): a rigid external body covering that provides support and protection

hexagrams (HEK-suh-grams): a star-shaped figure formed by two intersecting equilateral triangles

lithium-ion (LITH-ee-uhm EYE-on): referring to a type of rechargeable battery in which lithium ions move from the negative electrode to the positive electrode during discharge and back when charging

microstructure (MYE-kruh-struhk-chur): the fine structure (in a metal or other material) that can be made visible and examined with a microscope

mollusks (MOH-luhsks): animals with a soft body and no spine, often with a shell

polarization (poh-lur-uh-ZAY-shun): the action of causing something to acquire

polymer (POL-uh-mur): a compound made of small, simple molecules linked together in long chains of repeating units

receptors (ri-SEP-turs): organs or cells able to respond to light, heat, or other external stimulus and transmit a signal to a sensory nerve

silicone (SIL-uh-kuhn): a chemical element found in sand and rocks and used to make glass, microchips, and transistors

superhydrophobic (SOO-pur-hye-druh-foh-bik): repelling water to the degree that droplets do not flatten but roll off instead

Index

Show What You Know

1. What is biomimicry?
2. Why do cockleburs stick to clothing and dogs?
3. What substance on fish scales and eagle eyes creates a self-cleaning surface?
4. What are two products inspired by geckos?
5. What may be the strongest biological material on Earth?

Further Reading

Benyus Janine, *Biomimicry: Innovation Inspired by Nature*, Harper Perennial, 2002.

Mara, Wil, et al, *Innovations from Nature*, Cherry Lake Publishing, 2014.

https://asknature.org

About the Author

Robin Koontz is a freelance author/illustrator of a wide variety of nonfiction and fiction books, educational blogs, and magazine articles for children and young adults. Her 2011 science title, *Leaps and Creeps - How Animals Move to Survive*, was an Animal Behavior Society Outstanding Children's Book Award Finalist. Raised in Maryland and Alabama, Robin now lives with her husband in the Coast Range of western Oregon where she especially enjoys observing the wildlife on her property. You can learn more on her blog: robinkoontz. wordpress.com.

Meet The Author!
www.meetREMauthors.com

www.rourkeeducationalmedia.com

PHOTO CREDITS: Cover gecko © kongsky, gecko foot © Mr.B-king, cover velcro © svetlana55, burr © sumire8, kevlar © EVorona; page 4-5 © Nezrah; page 6 microscope © BrAt82, page 7 modern velcro © svetlana55; page 8-9 background photo © GiroScience; page 10-11 © ducu59us, paw closeup © beckart; page 12-13 static electricity © anigoweb, gecko © kongsky, page 14-15 gecko foot © Mr.B-king, TV © REDPIXEL.PL; page 16-17 main photo © Andrea Izzotti, suction cups © joesayhello, octopus on blue © Fotokon, on rocks © Nataliia Krasnenko; page 18-19 limpets on rock © Aloneontheroad, limpet underside © coxy58, goethite © Albert Russ, page 19 snail © Aleksandar Dickov; computer, phone © Alexey Boldin; page 20-21 water on lotus leaf © buddhawut, lotus inset © leisuretime70; page 22-23 insect molting © Norjipin Saidi, chitin molecule © sciencepics, shrimp shells © Eldred Lim, recycle symbol © barbaliss ; page 24-25 scuba diver © Daniel Wilhelm Nilsson, fish and fish scales closeup © n7atal7i, page 25 skeletal flowers © Kiet Van Nguyen; page 26-27 snake © Brian Goff hexagram © Vector.design; page 28-29 © Chris K Horne; page 30-31 © nevodka; page 32-33 illustration © Designua, shrimp eyes closeup © Ethan Daniels, polarized salt crystals © PRILL, human eye closeup © Milos Batinic; page 34-35 and 36-37 © Muhammad Naaim, page 37 inset photo © NASA; page 38-39 beetle © vblinov; page 40-41 full-length pangolin © Frank Booth, pangolin at night © Tallies, pangolin curled up © Positive Snapshot; page 42-43 wiper knob © WANWI17, windscreen and wipers © Ditty_about_summer; page 44-45 black road © Mags, cats eye road closeup © Dmitry Naumov, cat © By Maslowski Marcin   All images from Shutterstock.com except: page 4-5 inset © Christian Fischer https://creativecommons.org/licenses/by-sa/3.0/deed.en ; page 7 velcro inset © Pablo Alberto Salguero Quiles. https://creativecommons.org/licenses/by-sa/3.0/deed.en ; page 9 space suit courtesy of NASA; page 38 Dew bank bottle © Pak Kitae; page 41 Pangolin Renegade M backpack, © Pangolin®. www.mypangolin.com

Edited by: Keli Sipperley

Produced by Blue Door Education for Rourke Educational Media. Cover and Interior design by: Nicola Stratford   www.nicolastratford.com

Library of Congress PCN Data

Nature-Inspired Contraptions / Robin Koontz
(Nature-Inspired Innovations)
ISBN 978-1-64156-455-7 (hard cover)
ISBN 978-1-64156-581-3 (soft cover)
ISBN 978-1-64156-698-8 (e-Book)
Library of Congress Control Number: 2018930483

Rourke Educational Media
Printed in the United States of America, North Mankato, Minnesota